Roundy & Friends
Book 12

Andres Varela

Illustrations and Graphic Design by Carlos F. González
Co-Producer Germán Hernández
Second Edition
© 2019 Soccertowns® LLC

Remember this from the first time we met? We've completed the whole journey, and we've added more Soccertowns to the trip. In every country in the world, there are always more towns growing professional soccer teams – Atlanta and Orlando are two of them.

The team takes the train south from Atlanta to Orlando.
The train has glass windows all around so people can look outside. It also has a snack bar with a shaved ice machine plus many other delicious treats!

Orlando's actual population is under 300,000 people, but the metropolitan urban area, which includes four counties (Orange, Osceola, Seminole and Lake), has a population of over 2 million people!

Orlando is known as the theme park capital of the world with an estimated 65 million tourists visiting the city every year. The Orlando area is mainly wetlands, consisting of many lakes and swamps.

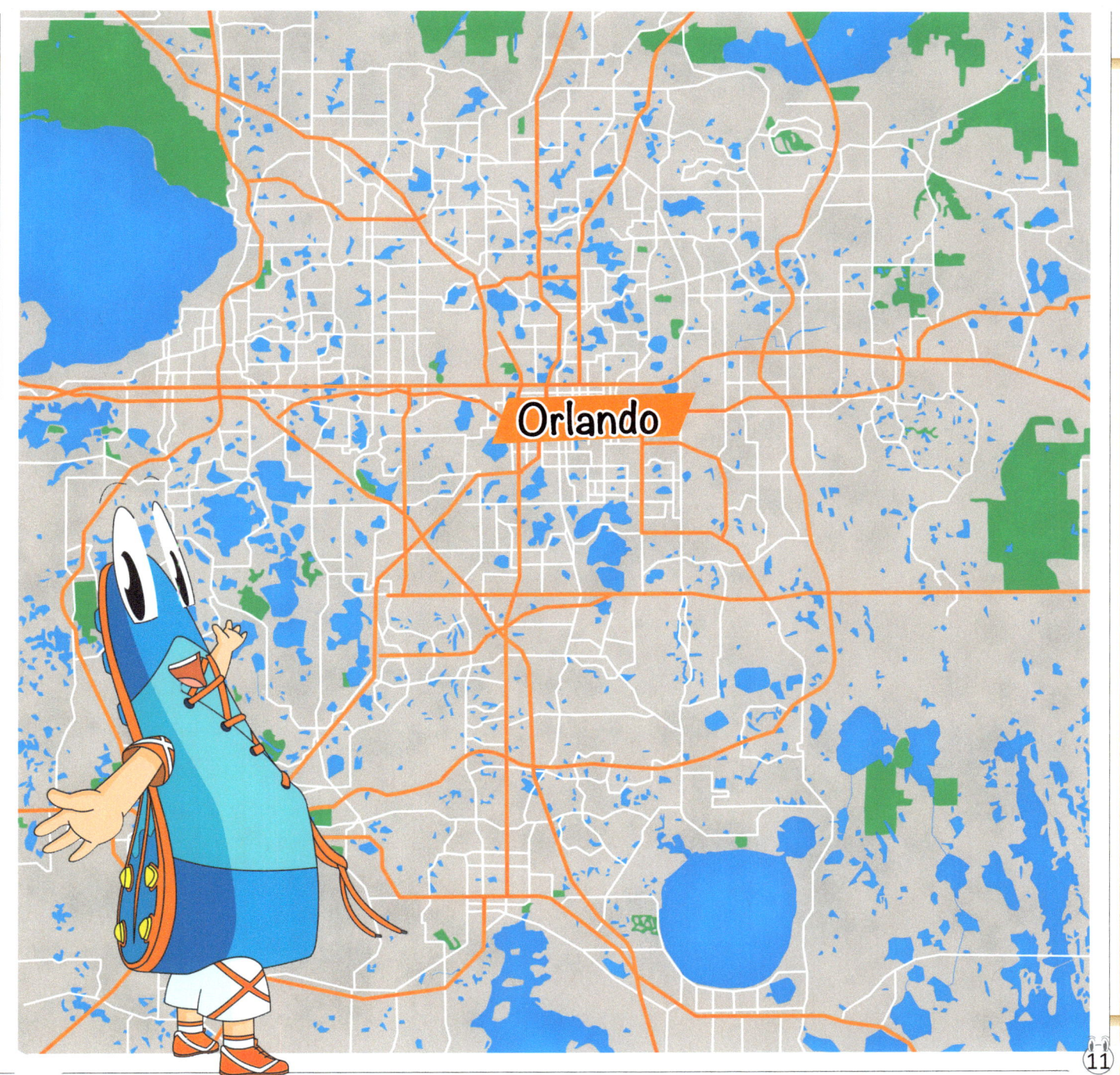

The first major theme park was built in 1971. Since then, Orlando experienced explosive growth, attracting millions of tourists and building the most amazing hoteling infrastructure in the whole world!

Orlando features thousands of Lakes. One of the biggest lakes is called Lake Eola, which is located near downtown.

Due to the ideal weather conditions for reptiles and insects to thrive, thousands of alligators and other wildlife live in the State of Florida.

Because there are so many lakes near Orlando, there are many fun things to do like riding an airboat! Airboats are shallow-draft boats powered by an aircraft engine, for use in swamps.
These boats don't damage the plants in the swamps.
"What if we run over an alligator," says Ben.
"Don't worry," Teo says, "the boat is made not to hurt it and just push it down into the water."

Orlando has the second largest number of hotel rooms in the United States with over 140,000 rooms - second only to Las Vegas.
The team spends a nice afternoon in the lazy river at one of the major hotels in the city.

"I like swimming against the current," says Jersey.

Another great attraction near Orlando are the beaches, which are on both sides of the state. The team decides to visit both the Gulf of Mexico, as well as the Atlantic beaches.

In the Gulf of Mexico, they enjoy Clearwater Beach, while in the Atlantic, they get to experience Cocoa Beach.

With Clearwater only an hour and 45 minutes away and Cocoa beach only an hour from Orlando, they can see the beautiful beaches on both coasts in one day!

The Gulf of Mexico beaches have some of the best sea shells in the world. The team collects some of these beautiful seashells. "Look at what I got," says Roundy. "They come in so many different colors." "I can hear the ocean in mine," says Shorty!

Also, many bird species live in the area. Teo loved them coming to visit them.

After lunch they decided to drive East to the other side of the State.
There are some spectacular bridges in Florida that allow both great views of the ocean and allow big boats to float under them.

Cocoa Beach is famous for its surfing waves. The team rents some surfboards to give it a try. Some of them get out of the water on the surfboard right away. Others spend more time swimming than surfing!

While Roundy is surfing, he imagines a shark coming to get him, but, in reality, shark attacks are extremely rare.

Teo tells the team, "It is more likely to get hit by lightning than to be attacked by a shark. Sharks don't spend much time near the beach as they like colder waters deep into the ocean." This put Roundy's mind at ease!

After they had a lot of fun surfing, they find a nice ice cream truck and enjoy eating ice cream.
While there, one of the lifeguards tells them that there was a storm coming, and it's best to get out of the beach and head inland.
Bringing heavy rain and strong winds, storms are very common in Florida. They typically leave as soon as they come.
The team gets in the hotel shuttle to head back to Orlando.

Orlando was a lot of fun, and it was the last town in the Eastern side of North America they visit.
In the next adventure they head North West to meet up with Thomas who spent a week driving from Toronto to Vancouver. Thomas will pick the team up at the airport in Vancouver, Canada so they can continue their adventure in the West Coast!

www.ingramcontent.com/pod-product-compliance
Lightning Source LLC
Chambersburg PA
CBHW042313280426
43661CB00101B/1211